"A Lifetime Meeting With My Guardian Angel"

(… In... Person... Book One, Part Three)

by N.I.S-->

ABELL PUBLISHING LLC

"A Once In A Lifetime Meeting With 'My' Guardian Angel" (… In... Person... Book One, Part Three)

~ Preface ~

I've become more and more fascinated with human history, and the more I consider my own, the more I realize the vast-- immeasurable amount of personal history that continually surrounds all-of-us in life, "Each Other's Stories!"

How Truly WONDROUS it is, to be able to share in the lives

of someone else, without having actually-been-there, to witness all the trials and tribulations, etc... that someone's passed thru, or gone through.

THANK GOD for the Writers-Authors, who battle their ways through the *painstaking efforts*, to craft a story... their story-- for all of us to be blessed with-- to read and experience--- As-If "we"... were THERE-WITH-THEM... all

along. With each step
they ever took, or would
and will take.

How fortunate are WE,
THE READERS and
RECEIVERS of these
many countless stories
told?

And when the story is
from a person's personal
history, it's *even better*
isn't it? For it is only
truly THEN, that we get
to RELATE with one
another, on the highest
level of connections
possible, from one

Human Being, to thee
other and back again.

How's THAT... for
reciprocation on a grand
scale? :--))

*It is for this very reason
that I write, craft and
share my own personal
history.*

Of course, *I'm doing this
backwards. Apparently*
(I'm told) I should have

become FAMOUS first, or WORLD RENOWNED, *before* I started sharing of *my own personal life's stories.*

They said to me, "Or you'll just be *a drop in the bucket, no different than anyone else out in reading and writing land.*"

Oh well, so beit then, if that is the case.

For those who don't read,
or care to read my books,
in lieu of my LACK of
FAME, NAME or
FORTUNE... tis THEIR
LOSS... due to their
choice... not mine or
yours. :--))

And so... On we go!

Thanks kindly always,
"For being here with me,
as I share my life's
journey's with you... as
crazy as they are, and

shall be-- *even more as we move forward*...

LOL-- you truly have... ***NO IDEA what we're IN FOR***! BUT--- if you read on... you shall surely see!

As I always say in these moments, "We shall see..."

~

Acknowledgments

~

Again, a big ***THANKS***!
to those who so
thoughtfully encouraged
me, in my pursuit of,
getting my stories written
and out-and-into the
hands of the reading
world and realm.

And, thanks so much ***to
ALL of MY READERS,***
for taking this journey
with me, and for-- ***your***

continued patronage!

Without you, *I do not exist.*

Please continue ***to share my stories with your families and friends in support of my writings...***

IF you would be... so kind.

~A Time Of Remembrance!~

I wish to thank the following people:

My wondrous amazing **Mom**! *Huggs n Love always Mom!*

God and Son! None of

this would have been possible, without *Them* in my life! They have always beenhere with me, and without fail!

A multitude of friends & acquaintances along the way! *Thanks kindly!*

And to ALL those, *who didn't just blow me off...*

Thanks kindly always! ! !

(N.I.S-->)

"... If you don't write it... it doesn't get written"

*"**Words** don't reach a page without the mind, heart, soul, spirit, as-well the **physical efforts by thee author** and thus- - the need for those who write!" (N.I.S-->)*

Published by:

Abell Publishing LLC--

17202 97th pl sw #B101

Vashon Island, Wa. 98070

 (E-Book & Paperback) ---

"*First Printing*" ---

Written By: (N.I.S-->)

Covers Designed in Collaboration by: Touqeer Shahid & (N.I.S-->)

Illustrations & Images by
(N.I.S-->)

~ ~ ~

TABLE OF CONTENTS

~ ~ ~

Another Adventure?...

Jailed... at Three Years of Age...

A Lasting Memory... A Scar from Parrot Street... Thanks A Lot... Tracy...

"Additionally"...

"Another Lil Tid Bit"...

"A Little More About Me, and What I'm Doing"...

1

"The Search... Is ON..."

It took me a bit of time searching every--house's--yard. I managed to do it... fairly quickly. I'd alternate from one house on our side to a house on thee other side... checking in every direction for her. One by one, until I reached the houses at the bottom of our street. The house on our side of the street, at the end, was the last one that I'd reach before catching a glimpse of something in my peripheral vision... across the street from where I was standing. Fear struck me to my core as I turned to see it. No!... No! This could not be! She could not be '*there*.' Suddenly I was having a very hard time swallowing. My mouth had gone instantly dry, and my heart began beating harder and faster as reality set in.

Time suddenly slowed to an eerie speed. I slowly turned my head the rest of the way around--- hoping I was not seeing what I thought I was seeing. It took just a moment of time to realize… *I was!*

It was ***that house, the one the people of our neighborhood were so fearful of. The house where they said, "someone lost their life, and where nobody was permitted to enter."***

As I looked across the street-- toward that dreadful place, a chill went through my skin and into my bones. A *movement* in the side yard to the right caught my eye. By focusing, I could (just barely) see through the tiny gaps that were in-between thee old wooden fence boards. My body began to shake. However, with the same kind of courage Harry

Potter always displays, I proceeded--- inching my way carefully across the street. I tried to make out what was back there. When I got to the curb, I stood there looking at the place. Primal fear began to overwhelm me. I took notice. The house was broken down. It looked like it had been abused for years, and later... abandoned. Weather and time had combined and rotted it to a slow... miserable... end.

The lawn was browned from exposure to sunlight- mixed with thee occasional rainfall and temperature changes that occurred for 'who knows how long.' The siding on the walls were a dark brown, aged color showing signs of weathering. A few of the windows had cross-hatched patterns... like most cottages. "I really like those--- cottages, and those styles of windows… 'Craftsman' is what they call them, I believe." Some of the siding boards were falling off. "I guess the nails hadn't lasted?"

I could see a garage (on the left side) while facing the house (directly) from the street. To the left of the garage, there was also a small side yard. Most of the houses in the neighborhood were the same design, only flipped or mirrored.

There was a gate on the right side with missing boards. The boards were attached in a vertical direction or bottom-to-top, which made it easy to enter. "The one to enter, sure as heck wasn't going to be me!" No way… No how! I would take the hard stance on this point! And right when I'd convinced myself that there was no way on Earth that I would be entering that place… guess what happened? You probably, already know...

It was the puppy. I could see her through the gaps between the fence boards. She was running back and forth... playing, it seemed. I felt my skin crawl, and, in fact... it was. Goosebumps spread from the tips of my toes to the top of my head, and... to thee end of each hair. It was the most terrifying feeling ever, to think for one moment that 'I' was going to have to go inside that creepy place... ***to get that puppy dog***.

Gulping deeply, I started walking

toward the gate to the side yard... where she was frolicking around.

       I arrived before the gate. I stood there a moment... looking it over. My heart was pounding so hard; I thought it would come completely out of my chest. I tried to swallow, but my saliva had stopped working. My mouth was as-dry-as-dry-could-be... like the sands of the Sahara.

       As I reached for the gate, a creaking noise came from behind me. I turned sharply, my heart jumping up and into my throat. My adrenaline was coursing through my veins like a speeding locomotive gone awry. Thankfully, it was just a loose board rubbing against another... due to the wind. It was kind of like the sound a cricket makes as it rubs its legs together... a chirping-scraping sound.

I was so scared. I don't even know if there was a word invented to adequately describe the feeling that swept over me!..."?""

I turned back,

facing the gate. I peered through the missing boards (just barely in time) to see the pup as she disappeared again–this time... around the corner of the house.

"What if *they* get her?" I thought. I have to save her. I'm going in!"

And so, with all the nerve I could muster, I propped myself up with my hands against the gate and lifted my right leg slowly--- putting it carefully through the missing board's opening and setting it down on the lawn inside. Next, I maneuvered my body

sideways to fit the gap,
slipping my right arm inside
and then squatting (slightly
enough...) to fit my head in
and through the slot,
followed by my chest,
releasing some air-- in order
to collapse it enough... to
make it through. It worked.
As I moved the rest of my
body through...
Rrrrrriiiiiiippppp!!! (The
sound of tearing) I looked
down quickly. A nail had
caught my pants (about mid-
thigh) and ripped them
slightly open. "Oh no! My
Mom's not gonna be happy
about that!"... oh, great!"

The most

important thing right now
was that 'I made it... I'm in!'

There I stood,
looking around. I began
shaking more... like a leaf--
on the branch of a tree... in
wind and rainstorm. The pup,
however, was nowhere to be
seen. I was frustrated.

"Where'd she
go this time?" I asked myself.
"Somewhere around the
corner... I saw her." My eyes
shifted and took in the sight
of the house again. It seemed
ten times larger than it did
only moments ago. I stood
there feeling rather small…
tiny actually.

I would have
to go around the corner to see
where she'd gone. I was
extremely nervous about
being there. Taking in some
deep breaths, I stepped
slowly towards the corner.
Each step became more
difficult than the one before.
My balance was excellent,
but I began to feel very weak.
My legs felt like they
weighed a million pounds.
"Why were they so heavy?"
They just wanted to collapse.
"What the heck's going on
here?" I frowned quizzically.
Legs or no legs, I'm not going
to stop!

I took a few

more steps and reached the corner. I was breathing hard. It was a battle to do this, but I kept on reminding myself what my Mom had said earlier, "If I catch her, I can have her, and she'll be mine forever." The reminder was all the encouragement I needed. Without hesitating further, I extended my right hand forward with my left trailing behind.

The siding felt *noticeably rough* to my fingers and palms. My hand grasped the corner, and my body reacted naturally; I took in a huge swallow... wondering what I would see.

It took everything I had in me to force myself to look around the corner... I had to! I had to see where she had gone. How else would I catch her to bring home? It was almost too much to bear, but I looked... regardless of my fears.

The tip of my nose reached the corner, and I was about to peek around it when a SOUND came, and SOMETHING JUMPED OUT! I immediately leaped backward, rolling my body against the wall with my left hand trying to maintain its grip, but I lost it and slipped to the ground. It was none

other than that darn puppy.
She was elated, jumping all
over the place and dodging
from side to side... like an
animal gone wild. She took
off around the corner again.

I jumped to
my feet quickly and chased
after her. It was a straight
shot to the backyard. I
stopped, looked over the area
carefully, my ears keen to
any sounds. Where was she
now? She was like Houdini.
She was nowhere in sight. I
sighed and placed my hands
on my hips as I looked
around. I wanted to find her,
but at the same time keep my
eyes on that house. I was

scared. I didn't notice any movements inside, but then I wasn't tall enough to see anyway... not even on my tippy toes. I heard another sound. "Ah-ha! There she is!" It was much harder than to catch her than I thought it would be. I was determined to bring her home. It was a dream to come true... but only *IF* I could catch her. I remember thinking to myself, "Why is she so dang hard to catch? Didn't she realize that my Mom said it was okay, so everything would be just fine?" I thought she'd be really happy... like me. She would finally have a home and a family that loves and adores her. No more having to beg for food, no more trying to find a place to sleep. We could play every day... all day... to our heart's content. How perfect would this be!..."?" I had it all worked out already, of course. I needed her to come to me.

"Come on, girl, come-ere! Come on, girl!" I patted my knees-- trying to bring her close enough to grab or to lunge for her. I tried this tactic over and over. Each time my enthusiasm grew, but she remained out of my reach. She ran to the fence, used her

nose to push a board aside,
and through it she went.
Poof! Gone! But not for long.

Within a
minute, she poked her head
back inside the fence and
stared at me. Was I supposed
to know what she wanted?
The bigger question was,
"What's on thee other side of
'that' fence?"

I walked
directly to thee opening. The
board was still swinging back
and forth. I stopped it from
swinging and moved it aside.
This allowed me to peer
through to see whatever was
on thee other side. I scanned

the yard once more and poked my head... carefully... through thee opening. It was a hillside. I noticed there was a familiar ground cover known as 'pickleweed or ice-plant' laying at the base of the fence and covering the whole side of the hill.

I poked my head through to spot the pup. I could see her clearly. I could see a lot more now, too...

I saw a long, steeply sloping hillside, and the house behind me was near the edge of it. The hillside was covered in pickleweed-- nothing but pickleweed. I'd never seen so much.

The hillside led down, and at the bottom... was this strange street. It wasn't 'just a street' like the one in front of our house. It was *a bunch of streets altogether and cars running both ways at the same time*. It had a large divider in the center that separated the cars traveling in opposite directions. It looked strange to me, but wow--- there sure were A LOT OF CARS down there!

The

pickleweed or ice-plant (if you're not familiar with it) is green, like a jade-plant petal, with 'almost' the same texture, but the petals aren't flatish like jade petals are; instead, each petal is long like a finger-- actually, as I recall... they're like prisms. A sort of elongated triangular cylinder... if that makes sense? Each finger of pickleweed is about three to five inches long and perhaps half to three-quarters of an inch in thickness. If you break it open, it's wet or juicy... but don't taste it. It doesn't taste good at all! I can tell you from personal experience and not a 'good' experience, I assure you. Each finger of pickleweed is attached to a vine that runs into the ground, in every direction imaginable. It reminds me of blackberry bushes in a way.

I focused on what I was seeing; an embankment covered in pickleweed and a bunch of strangely connected streets. But there weren't any houses... not one... and not on either side of the streets. I didn't understand it at all. I thought to myself, "Why aren't there any houses down there, and why are there so many cars?"

My attention now focused on the cars running back and forth, so I didn't notice the pup had run down the hill and was standing at thee edge of the streets. Sensing something, I thought, "Oh, man! I had best get down there before she tries to cross!" I felt fear rise up inside of me. This may not turn-out-well at all...

Off I went... sliding and jumping down the pickleweed to the streets below. The pup kept looking back at me as I was coming down the hill toward her. I must have looked like a total psycho. The hill was so steep I couldn't maintain my balance, falling, rolling, and bouncing and using leverage to try to get back on my feet. I somehow managed to steady myself before I hit the bottom.

"Would she stay there and allow me to get close enough to grab her? Or, would she take off the moment I get within reach?" All I could think of was "to get ahold of her and take her home."

I reached the bottom of the hill and stopped... dead-cold-frozen in my tracks...

2

"Frozen With Fear, At Thee Edge Of... Thee Interstate Highway..."

It was loud... very loud. A gust of wind grazed across my face, followed by another and--- another, and then... two or three together. It was so strong that it pushed me slightly off-balance—enough, so I had to regain my stance and take on a stronger one. It was the cars whipping past that made the wind and sound so terribly loud. As I stood there... they didn't lessen much at all.

       I stood there on the side of the streets, watching as all the cars were passing by. I was thinking to myself, "Wow, there are so many, why are there so many? Where are they all going?" I remained frozen in place, thinking about it. My concentration was interrupted. I realized *something was very wrong with this picture*.

       My eyes traced over thee area like a fine-toothed comb. In the

middle of the streets was a
short wall (a divider), and to
my utter dismay... there stood
the pup... right next to it.
She'd (somehow) gone right
through all the cars passing
by-- without my noticing, and
to the wall. This meant- I'd
have to go there too-- IF... I
was going to catch her. This
did not look good for me... or
for her. THIS was death
staring us, right in the face. I
looked to my left. I could see
all the cars were coming
toward me... very fast.

       I had to find
an opening to get to her, but
how was I going to get there
with all those cars coming at

once? Fear had slowly crept into me. I was breathing much faster. My heart was pounding harder and harder. I knew how fast I could run, but the cars were... much faster. I would have to time it just right *to run between the cars...* to get to her. I was REALLY SCARED, but nothing was going to ruin this. Nothing was going to stop me from getting to the pup and making her mine... NOTHING!!!

       I looked everything over again. I made my choice... I just needed to find the perfect moment... to-go-for-it!

I didn't have a clue what timing was, but I was determined to fulfill my dream. So, timing or not...

Looking left again, watching the cars pass by-- I felt certain... my plan was going to work. I spied *a gap between the cars*--- it's now or never...

My eyes fixated; I swayed forward and backward slightly... getting prepped.

As the cars got

closer, my heart was
pounding.

My adrenalin
kicked in. I took one more
look at the pup... she was
watching me. Time to go!
Taking a big breath-- I leaned
forward as the target car
passed by. The gap appeared-
-- I burst into the gap. Thee
other cars were not far behind
at all, so I ran as fast as I
could... as fast as my three-
year-old legs would carry
me...

I looked at the
cars following and noticed
the one closest to the dividing
wall. It was much faster than

thee others. My brain was screaming, "*I have to run faster... It's coming too fast... I'm not gonna make it... I'm gonna die...*"

My eyes shifted in the direction of the pup. Her neck was extended high, and I saw her focus shift from me to the quickly approaching car... and back again. She appeared very antsy... as she watched. It seemed like she sensed that... I was in jeopardy...

The car

beeped its horn. It was loud-- so loud; I felt like my head was about to explode. I needed to *leap*- so I wouldn't be struck by the car... from the side. I leaped with all the strength I had... and....thank goodness... I made it to the middle-- and just in the nick of time. My body smashed into the divider wall with such speed and force, I almost went over and onto thee other side. I had to catch my breath...

The pup drew

in next to me, and she rubbed against me over and over. She comforted me. I think it was her way... of hugging me.

I looked at the people (in their cars) as they passed by. They were looking at us 'strangely'… like we didn't belong there at all. Of course--- they were right... we didn't. No kids or animals belong on *an Interstate Highway.* This fiasco wasn't over... not just yet. In the middle of the highway, with cars flying past in every direction... we were *TRAPPED!*

The pup abruptly jumped over the divider. Once over, she stood there looking at me like she was waiting for me to jump over too. I moved forward, pressing my body against it so I could roll over it.
[Determination--- it's a tricky thing at times]

There wasn't any way-- shape or form, that would cause me to lose this pup. Not after all we'd just gone through together. No way, José! Wherever she went--- I was going too… period! I peered to my right, and I could see a bunch of cars coming FAST from thee opposite direction... the polar opposite!

She took off suddenly. I wanted to go too, but I couldn't... my legs would not allow me. I was alone... petrified... holding onto the divider for dear life.

Wind gusts from the cars felt stronger now, too. I held on tightly. I watched the pup as she turned back to look for me as she was crossing the streets. I think she knew I couldn't move by myself. Without hesitation... she came back for me. We'd cross *together*-- this time...

She gently took my wrist into her mouth (tenderly but firmly), and I knew she was going to be guiding me. She tugged, and I went right along with her. She successfully brought us to thee other side... safe at last--- but how would we get back?

I sat down on the grass along thee edge of the streets. Too scared to go any further, not even so much as another foot... in any direction. Just then, a car stopped near us.

A man and a lady were inside. They got

out and asked, "Hey, young man, what are you and your dog doing out on this road alone? Where are your parents? Where do you live? Do you live around here?" I didn't know what to say to them. They continued... "Are you lost? What's your phone number? What's your address? What are the names of your mother and father? How old are you?" It was dizzying. *I think I was in shock* as I sat there listening to them but not (truly) understanding them...

They tried to comfort me as much as they could, but even 'they' didn't know (exactly) what to do. The driver was constantly looking at the cars heading in both directions. It was obvious.... he was looking for *someone or something, but who... or what?*

As we were sitting there, alongside the highway, the passenger, a woman, crouched down. She spoke to me with a soft and comforting tone. It was a welcome moment amidst the cloud of stress and anxiety.

I watched the driver as he paced to and fro. It was very curious to me... his behavior. I wanted to

know what he was searching
for or wanted...

We were about to find out...

The dangerous path
Sheba and I took nearly cost
us our lives.

[Photo- Courtesy Google
Maps- Topographical-with
path by N.I.S-->]

3

"The Hand-Off..."

The driver saw it heading in the opposite direction and began waving to get its attention. I could see the cop stick his arm out the window and wave back... assuring him that he'd come back to us.

It wasn't long before the Police car pulled over and stopped... just behind the man's car.

There were two Policemen walking over to us. When they got close enough, one of them asked, "Is everything okay, Sir... Maam?"

He replied, "No sir, it's not okay. We found this boy and his dog in the middle of the freeway with nobody around them. No Parents, no family, no friends... they're on this highway alone, so we pulled over to see if we could be of service. The kid doesn't seem to know where his home is. So, we decided to stay here with them until we could flag one of you guys down. Do you need us for anything more? We were on our way home."

"Thanks for your help, and for being a good citizen," the policeman said. "If we could just get some information from you before you go? As a witness to whatever you saw, please?"

"Yes, of course, officers!" he replied.

*** ---[All of this is not verbatim--- I was only three years of age, so the words may have been different. This is a basic recollection, using common sense to piece things together as they may have been said.|---

After thee officers spoke with them, they went to leave, but not before assuring me that, "you and your dog will be... just fine. You're in good hands now."

The Policemen escorted the dog and me into their patrol car. The dog went in first, with me following. A Policeman buckled my seat belt and shut the door, and got in the front seat passenger side. As the driver started the car, he looked over to thee other officer and said, "You better call it in!"...

I remember sitting in the back seat of that police car and petting the puppy... MY puppy. She didn't seem worried at all. She just lay there on the seat with her neck stretched out... resting her chin on my thigh. I really loved that pup!

I could hear the police-car radio and the policeman speaking into that little thing in his hand… a microphone for the radio. It was a two-way radio system. He finished with the radio talk and turned to his partner, the driver. They both then turned in their seats to face us.

The driver asked me, "Do you know your home address, kid?"

"No, sir, I don't," I replied.

"Do you know the phone number for the house you live in? "No, I don't, sir." "What is your last name, young man?"

"Umm…" I was thinking, but it didn't work out. "I don't know, sir."

Thee officers were none-too-pleased with my answers and queried each other about *what to do next*. Just then, the passenger officer asked me, "Where did you come from? How did you get on the freeway--- this road?" I answered, explaining that, "I came down from there," as I pointed to thee other side of the streets... to thee embankment of pickleweed. "Hey, I know that neighborhood! I can take us there, and he can tell us which house is his!"

Off we went, but not before the passenger seat officer told me, "Don't

worry, kid, we know right
where to take you now."

(The journey (or better said)
the fiasco, was about to take
yet another crazy turn...)

The car lunged
forward, and I was sucked
into the back seat... along
with the puppy. I saw her put
her claw on the left side of
the seat, trying to grab thee
edge. The passenger cop was
looking out, over us, through
the back window for cars.
Away we went!

I peered out of
the window next to the pup.
There, I could see other cars

near us.

We pulled off
the streets (an off-ramp) and
onto another one. This new
street was going its own way.
At this point, I became...
even more lost, but I kept
hoping they'd find our house.
*They said they would after
all*, and besides... I was
getting really hungry. The
pup was panting and drooling
on my leg, and on the
backseat... time to find
home... or not...

4

"Lost, In Search Of-- Home... Another Adventure?"

The policemen were talking about something... I really didn't understand what they were discussing; I just sat there listening and petting MY puppy--- that NO ONE would EVER take away from me again... NOT... EVER!!!

We turned a

corner to the left. As we did, the passenger cop turned around and looked at me and said, "Okay, kid, this is the street where you were pointing to. You could have gotten on the freeway from here and made it to where we found you... with those people. Look around, kid! Do you see your house? Sit up real tall and see if you can see which house is yours. Just tell us when you see it, we'll stop and see if your parents are there." I replied, "Yes, sir."

I sat up as told-- looking around, side-to-side. Scanning all of the houses I could. Nothing seemed right to me. The car was moving too fast. I couldn't make heads or tails out of anything. Nothing looked 'familiar.' I was confused. It seemed like the right street, because it went down a hill, and then back up, and there were houses on both sides.... but I didn't see our house...

The police car continued driving slowly down the hill-- to the bottom, then up thee other side... until we reached the top. Feelings of sadness were beginning to wash over me, and I recall wondering if I was ever going to see my home again. I felt... genuinely lost.

The passenger policeman asked me again, "Do you see any houses you know? Does anything look familiar?" He was very hopeful. I answered that "the hill is like ours, but I don't see 'our house' anywhere." "Don't worry," he said, "We'll give it another try."

We made a U-turn at the top of the hill-- so that we could take another look. We passed the houses one by one, all the way down to the bottom of the street-- and then up thee other side--

just like last time, only this time, we were heading in thee opposite direction, yet still... I saw nothing familiar. I think I was too young to recognize things, or... what to look for. Regardless, we struck out, and the policemen were not about to waste any more time searching the neighborhoods. They wouldn't rely on a child's memory. They decided to take us to the station... The Police Station.

We had no idea what lay ahead of us. But food, water, warmth, and safety sure were. They tried to figure out 'who we were, where we came from, and *who our parents were--'* so they could return us to them as soon as possible. They assumed our parents would be *very worried about us by now*, especially for not having seen nor heard from us all this time. We were going to jail!... thee adventure continues...

5

"Jailed... At Three Years Of Age..."

Things were about to escalate...

When we reached the precinct, there were reporters everywhere. The City of San Diego was about to be charmed by a story a reporter would write... A boy and his dog. Word traveled like wildfire. Every news outlet wanted exclusive rights to the story. It was a real-life media frenzy.

I don't recall everything, but I do recall lights flashing from everywhere... all at once. Click after click after click. People talking loudly-- aggressively pushing each other around... tons of commotion. They were acting like crazed animals. The policemen were fending them off while attempting to answer their barrage of questions-- for thee officers, and many more... for me.

Meanwhile--- the policemen rushed me and the pup directly into the station, and to my utter displeasure-- as well as horror--- they split us up, placing the puppy into the jail cell, and me... outside of it. It was scary looking with its big iron bars. I sat down on the floor as close to her as the bars would allow... petting gently... saying softly, " I think we're in big trouble, girl. Pop's not gonna be happy at all! Oh, brother!" I sighed, waiting for whatever would come next...

The room was large. There were desks surrounding us. Some were smaller... some larger. The floor was concrete with a polished finish... a darkish gray color.

Looking at the cell, there were really big steel bars that came right up and out of the floor. They traveled vertically, floor to ceiling. The bars must have been an inch thick, with perhaps four inches of space between each one. They were all the way around the cell. The floor was hard and painfully cold. Interestingly... 'I' **wasn't** the one placed inside that cage... it was the puppy. In looking back, I suspect they wanted to keep her contained.

One of the policemen brought me a blanket to sit on. I spread it out on the floor, allowing me to lay down as close to her as possible. Lying on my left side, I slipped my arm under the bars and into the cage. I had a natural sense of caring and compassion. (Nice to know... in looking back)

She joined me and placed her chin on top of my arm. We stayed that way... for as long as I can recall.

In the meantime, a huge crowd of people had gathered outside...

trying to get in. They wanted *photos, and to get the story for the evening editions of their issues, as well the mornings.*

Word traveled fast! It was a... true... media... frenzy-- and in those days... it was **BIG NEWS**. The headlines might've read... something like this:

"Boy Found on Freeway... Alone With Dog" -or perhaps-

"A Lost Boy and His Dog" -or something catchy like that.

You know how the media can be! It was a story, sure to capture the hearts and souls of the readers.

They really played it up, placing it on **The Front Page** of every paper in the area. I'm not sure if it was on television or not... it probably was. I saw thee article once, a short time after that, then again when my Mom brought it out to show me, and once again (fifty or so) years later, right after my wondrous Parents *lost their lives...* (That was in the year two thousand and fifteen). Losing their lives **wasn't due**

to natural causes either -I can tell ya-, but that's *another story...* one that I'll be writing some day in the not-so-distant future... God willing and permitting).

At the police station--- lying there on the cold concrete floor with my arm inside the jail cell, the puppy's head lying on my arm, can you imagine? What a photo op for the press boy howdy… did they ever jump at the chance to capture it! Now I know how animals at the zoo feel when people come around to gawk at them and capture them in photographs–being put on display for oh so many different reasons. Is there always a legacy surrounding such intentions? I truly wonder!..."?"

They came in droves, making a ton of noise--- all of them fighting for positions closest to the puppy and me. The puppy was not happy about it, she warned them growling, but they didn't listen... they never do... do they?

The Policemen were trying to control the reporters and their crew who were (fiercely) asking and demanding

questions of the Police. This
went on for quite some time.

They were
then given 'the go-ahead' to
ask me questions--- 'I' mostly
could not answer. I was
extremely shy. I didn't know
what to say -or how to
answer. All I wanted was to;
"just go home with my puppy
and celebrate our new lives
together... forever... as a
family."

-----[I'll have to see if I can
dig up thee article and photos
from the newspaper. I have
them 'somewhere safe.'
Which translates to, I may
never find them again. Oh,

the treasures!]-----

The rest is a blur for whatever reason, but one thing that I do know for sure:

'S*omeone or something'* guided me across the freeway that day, and it wasn't *'just the dog'* I'm speaking of here. It was as if, **"Someone had pushed me forward at the last moment, and was running alongside me, slightly behind--- but close enough to give me that final SHOVE when I thought I wasn't going to make it."**

It's, "Thank goodness we were both kept safe while crossing the freeway. We easily could have been run over and killed by the cars." Was this the result of a true-to-life Guardian Angel? And can you imagine...

What absolutely terrible news it would have been for my Parents to receive.

Thankfully, we both lived-- and thanks to *the hard work and efforts of the Police and Media,* we (later) were returned home to my Parents... alive and able

to tell the story... ***some fifty-
something years later***.
Strange how time passes by
so quickly... isn't it?

Life seems to
have a way of working things
out-- it seems, but at other
times one might look back
and wonder... "How they
managed to make it this far? I
sure do!" Hindsight 20-20...

I happen to
know there were forces
beyond our realm working to
make sure I was kept safe.
For whatever reason--- I do
not know, but hopefully... I
will do my part as intended
for me. God has my back,

and so does one special Guardian Angel. I am so very grateful for my life... even with the devastating and crushing moments that followed... throughout my lifetime. Those stories and they are many... shall follow in this series of books. Truly, I tell you...

"We'd be best off--- counting our blessings!" Dontcha think? We and our crazy lives, eh? I'll just bet 'you' also have a story or two to tell! Haven't you? Why not share them with the rest of us? After all, someone wise once stated that ***"Everyone loves a good*** *story!"* I look forward to sharing more of mine. It just gets crazier and crazier. So I've been told.

--- Oh! Wait a sec; there's One More Thing-- that Happened on Parrot Street...

6

"A Lasting Memory... A Scar From Parrot Street... Thanks A Lot Tracy!"

There were, indeed, some really crazy moments back on good ol` Parrot Street... for sure. I got another set of stitches from my 'friend?' Tracy. We were arguing over one of his toys, a fire truck. The fire truck was about two feet long, made out of metal, and red with a white extension ladder on top. The truck was covered with all the trimmings. It was long enough for us kids to sit on and ride around using our legs. (Kind of like thee old Flintstones cartoon characters did in those cars with the stone wheels). What a great show that was!!! It was the coolest thing.

Well, on this particular day, he got angry with me, picked up that fire truck, and threw it in thee air right at me. Thankfully, I had great reflexes, so when I saw it coming, I bent down to avoid being hit directly in the face. But I didn't bend down far enough because it struck me right on the ear, splitting it open and making me bleed. That was not going to end well for my friend Tracy... which it didn't.

When I reached up and touched my ear, I felt something wet and warm. I brought my fingers to where I could see them, and they were covered in blood--- not just anyone's blood... MINE! This enraged me the moment I saw it and realized what it was. My fists clenched as I looked at Tracy, and then, before I knew it, I let him have it...

SMACK... right in the nose! This, of-course, got me into more trouble... instead of the sympathy I'd hoped for. "KIDS!!!" That is the first **punch** that I ever threw in my life, but it sure as heck wouldn't be the last, I'll tell ya, and none of them was my fault-- I promise... really... I do!

Now then, that was on Parrot Street, which also painted a picture of what might be construed as "the beginnings of a long life of trouble... with a **BIG "T."** I can share with you here and now... it had only... just... begun. Ahem! Moving forward...

A short time after all this happened and things calmed down from the media frenzy, we moved to a new house-- on **Mt. Everest Boulevard**, where... *yours truly,* would find himself getting into-- *even BIGGER TROUBLE*... umm--- (totally innocent look now) something to do with fire... yet again. Fire fascinated me. Our move to Mt Everest would surely make that a reality-- on several counts--- *but just wait till you hear what happened when we moved from Mt. Everest... to Mt. Augustus Ave... oh*

boy!*...*

Boy oh boy howdy… I'll tell ya, "If there was one thing I seemed to be on my way to perfecting - or becoming great at, it was... "getting myself into trouble." ***Trouble*** would find me... wherever I was and wherever I'd go. It was relentless... it still is-- to this very day. You'll see what I mean later in the series--- after all, "We're just getting started here..."

~ ~ ~

"Additionally..."~ ~
~

Looking back-- recalling and reliving all of these crazy memories amazes me, honestly.

What a recall we have up there in those "storage containers" that sit... resting on our shoulders.

My goodness, the weight of it is eh!..."?"

We must have some wondrously strong shoulders to carry ALL OF "OUR LIFE'S MEMORIES... as-well-as burdens.

No wonder they say, "When we meet our maker upstairs--- it's going to be like watching a fantastically-articulated-symphony-like moment in time." Makes perfect sense to me!

"A Funny

Thing Occurred To Me After All Of This..."

After all of the recalling-- it occurred to me that, "The more I struggled, but prevailed to recall... to share...

*The **MORE** I found myself... **ABLE** to recall **even more!!!***

And isn't it strange how that works? (smiling)

I quite enjoy stumbling onto things like that!

But then again-- "That's always been... the way *that* **"I" am.**

I suck up information-- **Like There's NO Tomorrow for real!**

I also-- ASK QUESTIONS IF I ever feel the need... which I do a lot. It's all good, in

my humble opinion, and thankfully, "My Mom" was always willing to answer my never-ending line of questions!

And YOU THINK... TWENTY QUESTIONS was a LOT to have to answer? ahaha! Or as my Mom would say, "Hah!"

Oh-- but

here's a (perhaps) funny lil' tidbit! (Sorry, Mom! hehehe--- wicked-little-boy-grin!)..

~ ~ ~

"Another Lil' Tidbit..." ~ ~ ~

My poor, poor Mother! God rest her dear soul!...

I had a ZILLION questions AT ALL TIMES... I doubt (seriously) if even ONE DAY passed, that I hadn't bothered my Mom, as she was "trying" to read her books. (She was an **ABSOLUTELY VORACIOUS READER...** *devouring four to seven novels at a time. (Yepperz-- all at once).*

She'd sit on her office couch, one of her office chairs, or her

*favorite reading chair...
out in the living room.*

     *Of-course--
RIGHT NEXT TO
WHEREVER SHE WAS...
sat an ASHTRAY. (She
was also a MAJOR
CHAIN SMOKER--
smoking three-to-four
PACKS per day).
Amazing-- her lungs
were as clear as anyone
who had never smoked in
their lives. (GREAT
GENES-- IMMUNE
SYSTEMS in our family).*

*Anywho--
I'd come to Mom, she'd
be reading as always.
And so-- what would "I"
do? (Ever heard the
word NAG? Well-- I
DIDN'T NAG...) I just...*

*Ever so
gently-- and so very
KINDLY... "Tugged" on
her sleeve... tug, tug...
"Mom?"*

*(Wait a sec
for her to answer...)*

Tug, tug,

tug..."Ahem... Mom?"

(Wait a sec more...)

(Getting impatient here...)

"AHEM!!! TUG TIG TUGGGGG!!! MOM!!!"

And THAT would do it... she'd DROP her book to her lap, while at the very same time turning SHARPLY to look directly at me, and ASK,

"WHAT IS IT--- FOR HEAVEN'S SAKE???"

Smiling--- IT ALWAYS WORKED, and I ALWAYS GOT TO ASK!! But I don't mind telling you...

*SOMETIMES-- she'd **MAKE ME WAIT... FOR--- EVVVVERRRRRR!!!***

*LOL Okay-- okay, **A LITTLE BIT** dramatic... JUST a lil!*

*(winks... HEY! Let's get to **Mt. Everest Blvrd... shall we?**)*

*For **THIS MOMENT IN TIME...** fondly... adieu. . . **Wait a sec... there's one more thing I decided to share... "it's about me... what I'm doing..."***

~~ A Little More About Me, And What I'm Doing... ~~

This is another thing that I am doing at this time-- (It's very personal, but since we are on this journey together, I thought to myself, "Why not continue sharing with everyone who's kind enough to read my stories, and hopefully enjoy them?" So here I am to do so... more...)

I hope you will enjoy my Third Story in this particular series of mine. You can be assured, there shall be many more "Series" and differing Genres coming soon as well. (smiles softly... looking forward!)

The next in this series shall be, "Book Two, Part One, Part Two and Part Three." I have written them already, and will be, (as I have been doing thus far) getting them, one-by-one to my Editor, and then designing the front and back covers, handing them to my Graphic Artist "Touqe" to bring to life for our new books ahead, and then to publish time.

I always add my Forwards and Acknowledgements AFTER getting each book back from my Editor Val. Hoping to stay with formatting guidelines as we go.

I won't kid you all about becoming a "Published Author".. IF that is REALLY something you truly wish to do, or your heart, soul and spirit demand of you as mine do of me. Here's *The Truth About Becoming a "Published Author-Writer."*

Becoming a Published Author-Writer...

It takes STANCE.
Personal, God given,
STANCE. You are ON
YOUR OWN in this
quest, and you HAVE TO
FACE THE MUSIC of
THAT REALITY before
you even THINK to sit
down and take on the
quest of becoming the
Published Author.

I once stated to my
Mother, who wished for
me to write since I was
six years of age...
already a story teller. I

had QUITE thee imagination she always said and boasted about me-- her youngest and most treasured and adored child.

Later in life when I was considering "sharing my writings" I stated to my Mom that I was and her advice, "Learn the craft."

I frowned. "Learn the -- craft--?" LOL, what a LAUGH I thought. My thinking was, "Why do these people always have to make SO MUCH MORE out of something, than NEED to be. Like the use of words, why do we NEED to use words that confuse others, but appear above one's vocabulary, yet not above others? Why not just use Layman's terms always? Isn't SIMPLE talk easier to understand and thus relate too?" I thought my line of thinking was quite...

SPOT ON! Wasn't it?

I never saw the need for (as I say) "flowering up" something, that really didn't need to be. It's like in the political arena, they DRIVE ME UP A WALL. WHY they cannot seem to manage to ANSWER A QUESTIONS ASKED... DIRECTLY... is so far beyond my ability to grasp, I haven't the words. But it drives me NUTZ. I just want to strangle them, or smack em on the back, as-if their are choking on something and need that, to GET IT OUT... for crying out loud... SAY WHAT YOU MEAN, don't BEAT AROUND THE DARN BUSH!!! PLEASE!!! LOL

That's how "I" see it. I am not one FOR THAT mentality or behavior. I say exactly what needs to be said, and IF someone asks me a question, "I answer directly right back!" It shocks them that I do. People SEEM to expect the beating around the bush way of answering anymore. And when they find someone like me, who answers instantly, and directly right back... they think "I'm angry or mad" at them. Good grief Charlie Brown!... Get OVER IT! :--))

So back to becoming a Published Author-Writer:

It's VERY VERY VERY HARD WORK! I cannot emphasize that enough. I had NO IDEA how much WORK it actually is. And I am NOT trying to detour you whatsoever. Please do not consider that at all. What I am doing is, Giving You, 100% pure honesty... directly. Along with my thoughts of course. I do THINK and CONTEMPLATE A LOT and therefore I AM... a

*"?" Thinker, and a
Contemplator! Yep,
that's me!*

Writing takes:

*... Sitting ourselves down
in that chair, at that desk
or table or space, and
putting the pen, pencil,
marker, paintbrush,
quill, typewriter,
keyboard, voice program
TO TASK. And doing so,
beginning at A and
working our way all the
way till we reach Z.*

Beginning to End. And let me tell you, from my personal perspective, when I enter those last wondrous words, "Thee End"... the feeling of relief, is instantly felt and this feeling of having fought and won the wickedest of battles, and struggled my way, persisting with raw determination to reach my goal, thee end of my quest, and a story poured out on paper or screen file. Is the GREATEST

FEELING OF SUCCESS
I can fathom
experiencing.

Was it WORTH ALL I
went through to finally
reach that place? You
better believe it was and
IS. It always is. :--))
You'll see... IF you take
on the question yourself.

My greatest struggle
personally, is always the
same... "Getting myself
to SIT IN "THE

WRITING CHAIR" at my "WRITING DESK", yes I actually HAVE... a desk specifically FOR... "My Writing."

But when I can finally get myself IN THAT CHAIR... It's SUDDENLY.... -- ON --! And the writing commences as-if... I had never stepped away at all. LOL Strange to me, how THAT works. Ahh well, such are the ways of things we don't truly

*understand. Only the
Father does. :--))*

*Every human being HAS
a STORY unique to
everyone else's. Truly
Unique! And so with that
stated, I commend you to,
WRITE WRITE WRITE
and share yours.*

*We'll be the fortunate
ones when we get to read
from your hand, mind,
heart, soul and spirit.*

Please do... kindly always (N.I.S-->)

I have penned, written, drawn, and designed three articles that I will submit to:

1- The Scientific World Journal

2- American Journal Of Science

*The first
two...submissions are:*

**1--"The
Truth Behind Global
Warming"**

**2-- "How
Light Truly
Travels; Einstein
Was Wrong"**

As for the
3rd...

**"We shall
see..."**

Kindly

always,

(N.I.S-->)

*... I'll see
you's once again, when
we move forward into...*

**Book
Two, Part One. . .**

Or...

**As thee
adventures...**

continue.

..